Delivering Success The Power of Effective Supply Chain Management

Dennis

Copyright © [2023]

Title: Delivering Success The Power of Effective Supply Chain Management
Author's: Dennis

All rights reserved. No part of this publication may be reproduced, stored in a retrieval system, or transmitted in any form or by any means, electronic, mechanical, photocopying, recording, or otherwise, without the prior written permission of the publisher or author, except in the case of brief quotations embodied in critical reviews and certain other non-commercial uses permitted by copyright law.

This book was printed and published by [Publisher's: **Dennis**] in [2023]

ISBN:

TABLE OF CONTENT

Chapter 1: Introduction to Supply Chain Management   07

Understanding the Concept of Supply Chain Management

Evolution and Importance of Supply Chain Management

Benefits of Effective Supply Chain Management

Chapter 2: Key Components of Supply Chain Management   13

Procurement and Sourcing

Inventory Management

Warehousing and Distribution

Transportation and Logistics

Demand Planning and Forecasting

Chapter 3: Strategies for Effective Supply Chain Management   23

Lean Supply Chain Management

Agile Supply Chain Management

Just-in-Time (JIT) Supply Chain Management

Efficient Consumer Response (ECR)

Vendor-Managed Inventory (VMI)

Chapter 4: Technology and Automation in Supply Chain Management   33

Role of Technology in Supply Chain Management

Supply Chain Management Software and Tools

Internet of Things (IoT) in Supply Chain Management

Robotics and Automation in Supply Chain Processes

Chapter 5: Key Performance Indicators (KPIs) in Supply Chain Management   41

Importance of KPIs in Measuring Supply Chain Performance

Commonly Used KPIs in Supply Chain Management

Setting and Tracking KPIs for Supply Chain Success

Chapter 6: Supply Chain Risk Management   48

Identifying and Assessing Supply Chain Risks

Strategies for Mitigating Supply Chain Risks

Building Resilience in the Supply Chain

Crisis Management and Business Continuity Planning

Chapter 7: Sustainability and Ethical Considerations in Supply Chain Management   56

Sustainable Supply Chain Management Practices

Ethical Sourcing and Fair Trade

Corporate Social Responsibility in the Supply Chain

Environmental Impact and Green Supply Chain Initiatives

Chapter 8: Collaboration and Integration in Supply Chain Management   65

Importance of Collaboration in Supply Chain Management

Building Strong Supplier Relationships

Collaborative Planning, Forecasting, and Replenishment (CPFR)

Supply Chain Integration and Coordination

Chapter 9: Future Trends and Innovations in Supply Chain Management — 73

Industry 4.0 and the Digital Supply Chain

Artificial Intelligence and Machine Learning in Supply Chain

Blockchain Technology in Supply Chain Management

Predictive Analytics and Big Data in Supply Chain Optimization

Chapter 10: Case Studies in Effective Supply Chain Management — 81

Successful Supply Chain Management Practices in Retail Industry

Supply Chain Excellence in Manufacturing Sector

Supply Chain Innovations in E-commerce and Online Retail

Global Supply Chain Management in Multinational Corporations

Chapter 11: Conclusion and Key Takeaways — 90

Recap of Important Concepts Covered in the Book

Lessons Learned and Key Takeaways for Effective Supply Chain Management

Final Thoughts on the Power of Effective Supply Chain Management

Chapter 1: Introduction to Supply Chain Management

Understanding the Concept of Supply Chain Management

Supply chain management (SCM) is a critical aspect of business operations, particularly in the field of industrial engineering. It is the process of effectively managing the flow of goods, services, information, and finances from the point of origin to the point of consumption. In today's complex and interconnected global economy, a well-executed supply chain can provide a competitive advantage for businesses across various industries.

For industrial engineers, understanding the concept of supply chain management is essential as it enables them to optimize processes, reduce costs, and enhance overall operational efficiency. SCM involves the coordination and integration of various activities, including procurement, production, transportation, warehousing, and distribution. By effectively managing these activities, industrial engineers can ensure a smooth flow of materials and information throughout the supply chain, minimizing bottlenecks and maximizing productivity.

One of the key principles of supply chain management is the concept of value creation. This involves identifying and delivering value to customers while minimizing costs and waste. Industrial engineers play a vital role in analyzing and optimizing the different stages of the supply chain to achieve this objective. By understanding customer needs and preferences, they can design efficient processes that align with market demands, resulting in improved customer satisfaction and increased profitability.

Another important aspect of supply chain management is collaboration. In today's interconnected world, businesses cannot operate in isolation. Collaboration with suppliers, manufacturers, distributors, and customers is crucial for a successful supply chain. Industrial engineers can facilitate effective collaboration by implementing information systems, establishing communication channels, and fostering strong relationships with key stakeholders. By working together, the supply chain partners can share information, reduce lead times, and respond quickly to changes in demand or supply.

Furthermore, supply chain management is not a static process. It requires continuous monitoring, evaluation, and adaptation to meet evolving market dynamics. Industrial engineers need to leverage data analytics and technology to gain insights into supply chain performance, identify areas for improvement, and make informed decisions. By continuously optimizing the supply chain, businesses can enhance their competitiveness, reduce costs, and deliver products and services more efficiently.

In conclusion, understanding the concept of supply chain management is essential for industrial engineers. It enables them to effectively manage the flow of goods, services, information, and finances throughout the supply chain, optimizing processes, minimizing costs, and enhancing overall operational efficiency. By embracing the principles of value creation and collaboration, industrial engineers can create a competitive advantage for businesses in the field of industrial engineering. Continuous monitoring, evaluation, and adaptation are key to ensuring ongoing success in supply chain management.

Evolution and Importance of Supply Chain Management

Supply chain management has undergone significant evolution over the years, transforming from a mere logistics function to a critical strategic element for businesses across industries. In today's globalized and interconnected world, effective supply chain management is of paramount importance for organizations aiming to gain a competitive edge and deliver success. This chapter aims to explore the evolution and highlight the importance of supply chain management, particularly for individuals in the field of industrial engineering.

The evolution of supply chain management can be traced back to the early 20th century when businesses started recognizing the need for efficient coordination and integration of various activities involved in the movement of goods. Initially, the focus was primarily on transportation and warehousing, with limited consideration given to other aspects such as procurement and demand forecasting. However, with technological advancements, increased globalization, and changing consumer demands, supply chain management has evolved into a multi-dimensional discipline encompassing a wide range of activities.

Today, supply chain management involves the seamless integration of procurement, production, logistics, and customer service functions, among others. It encompasses the entire lifecycle of a product, from raw material sourcing to the final delivery to the end consumer. Supply chain professionals are responsible for optimizing processes, minimizing costs, reducing lead times, managing inventory levels, and ensuring customer satisfaction, all while maintaining sustainability and ethical practices.

For industrial engineers, understanding supply chain management is crucial as it directly impacts the efficiency and productivity of manufacturing processes. By applying their knowledge of process optimization, data analysis, and system design, industrial engineers can contribute significantly to enhancing supply chain performance. They can identify bottlenecks, streamline operations, implement lean principles, and leverage technology to drive continuous improvement throughout the supply chain network.

Moreover, industrial engineers play a vital role in ensuring the smooth flow of materials, information, and resources across the supply chain. They collaborate with various stakeholders, including suppliers, manufacturers, distributors, and retailers, to create value and deliver products to the market in a timely and cost-effective manner.

In conclusion, the evolution of supply chain management has transformed it into a critical discipline with far-reaching implications. Whether you are a practitioner, student, or enthusiast in the field of industrial engineering, understanding the importance of supply chain management is essential for success. This chapter will delve deeper into the intricacies of supply chain management, exploring key concepts, best practices, and real-world examples to equip you with the knowledge and skills necessary to excel in this dynamic field.

Benefits of Effective Supply Chain Management

In today's highly competitive business landscape, effective supply chain management plays a pivotal role in achieving operational excellence and delivering success. Supply chain management encompasses the coordination and integration of various activities involved in the procurement, production, and distribution of goods and services. This subchapter aims to explore the numerous benefits that effective supply chain management can bring to organizations across all industries, with a specific focus on the industrial engineering niche.

1. Increased Efficiency and Cost Reduction: Implementing effective supply chain management practices streamline processes, reduce waste, and enhance operational efficiency. By optimizing inventory levels, minimizing lead times, and improving production planning, organizations can significantly reduce costs associated with inventory holding, transportation, and warehousing.

2. Enhanced Customer Satisfaction: An efficient supply chain ensures that products are delivered to customers in a timely manner, meeting their expectations and demands. By effectively managing the supply chain, organizations can improve order fulfillment rates, reduce delivery times, and provide accurate and reliable tracking information, ultimately leading to increased customer satisfaction and loyalty.

3. Improved Collaboration and Communication: Effective supply chain management fosters collaboration and communication among various stakeholders, including suppliers, manufacturers, distributors, and customers. By establishing strong relationships and sharing relevant information, organizations can enhance transparency, reduce lead times, and respond quickly to changes in demand or supply.

4. Better Risk Management: Supply chains are vulnerable to various risks, such as disruptions in transportation, natural disasters, or supplier issues. By implementing effective supply chain management practices, organizations can identify potential risks, develop contingency plans, and minimize the impact of disruptions, ensuring continuity of operations.

5. Innovation and Competitive Advantage: A well-managed supply chain enables organizations to respond quickly to market trends, customer demands, and technological advancements. By leveraging supply chain data and analytics, organizations can identify opportunities for innovation, improve product quality, and gain a competitive edge in the market.

6. Sustainability and Social Responsibility: Effective supply chain management promotes sustainable practices, including ethical sourcing, waste reduction, and carbon footprint reduction. By incorporating sustainability into the supply chain, organizations can enhance their corporate social responsibility image, attract environmentally conscious customers, and comply with regulatory requirements.

In conclusion, effective supply chain management offers a multitude of benefits to organizations across all industries, including industrial engineering. From increased efficiency and cost reduction to enhanced customer satisfaction and innovation, organizations that prioritize effective supply chain management gain a competitive advantage and drive success in today's dynamic business environment.

Chapter 2: Key Components of Supply Chain Management

Procurement and Sourcing

In the ever-evolving landscape of supply chain management, procurement and sourcing play a pivotal role in ensuring the success of an organization. These two interconnected functions are the heart and soul of any industrial engineering operation. In this subchapter, we will explore the significance of procurement and sourcing, their key principles, and their impact on delivering success in the field of industrial engineering.

Procurement refers to the process of obtaining goods and services from external sources, while sourcing involves identifying and selecting the most suitable suppliers for these goods and services. The ultimate goal of procurement and sourcing is to acquire high-quality products at the best possible price, while also maintaining strong relationships with suppliers.

Effective procurement and sourcing strategies can make or break an organization's supply chain. By identifying reliable suppliers and negotiating favorable contracts, industrial engineers can ensure a steady and uninterrupted flow of materials, components, and equipment. This, in turn, helps streamline production processes, reduce costs, and enhance product quality.

One of the key principles of procurement and sourcing is the importance of strategic partnerships. By collaborating closely with suppliers, industrial engineers can gain valuable insights into market trends, technological advancements, and industry best practices. These partnerships foster innovation, improve product design, and enhance overall supply chain efficiency.

Another crucial aspect of procurement and sourcing is risk management. Industrial engineers must carefully evaluate potential risks associated with suppliers, such as financial instability, quality control issues, or geographical challenges. By diversifying suppliers and implementing contingency plans, organizations can mitigate risks and ensure business continuity.

In today's globalized marketplace, sustainability has become an integral part of procurement and sourcing strategies. Industrial engineers are increasingly focusing on environmentally friendly practices, ethical sourcing, and social responsibility. By prioritizing sustainability, organizations not only contribute to a better future but also enhance their reputation and attract socially conscious customers.

In conclusion, procurement and sourcing are critical elements of effective supply chain management in the field of industrial engineering. By employing strategic partnerships, risk management, and sustainable practices, organizations can optimize their procurement and sourcing processes, leading to improved operational efficiency, reduced costs, and ultimately, delivering success in the ever-competitive industrial engineering niche.

Inventory Management

Inventory management is a crucial aspect of effective supply chain management in the field of industrial engineering. It plays a vital role in ensuring the smooth flow of materials and goods throughout the supply chain, from suppliers to manufacturers to distributors and, ultimately, to the end customers. This subchapter aims to provide a comprehensive understanding of inventory management and its significance in achieving success in the supply chain.

The primary objective of inventory management is to strike a balance between ensuring adequate stock availability to meet customer demand while minimizing holding costs and the risk of obsolescence. By effectively managing inventory, companies can optimize their operations, reduce costs, and enhance customer satisfaction.

One key concept in inventory management is the Economic Order Quantity (EOQ). EOQ refers to the optimal quantity of inventory that should be ordered to minimize total holding and ordering costs. It involves finding the optimal balance between the costs of carrying excess inventory and the costs associated with placing frequent orders for small quantities. By calculating the EOQ, companies can determine the ideal order size that minimizes costs and maximizes operational efficiency.

Another important aspect of inventory management is the implementation of advanced technologies such as barcode systems, radio-frequency identification (RFID), and inventory management software. These technologies enable companies to accurately track and manage inventory levels, reduce manual errors, and improve overall visibility and control over the supply chain.

Furthermore, inventory management techniques such as Just-in-Time (JIT) and Vendor-Managed Inventory (VMI) have gained popularity in recent years. JIT involves receiving inventory just in time for production or distribution, reducing the need for excess inventory storage. VMI, on the other hand, involves suppliers managing inventory levels at the customer's location, further streamlining the supply chain and reducing costs.

Effective inventory management also requires forecasting customer demand accurately. By analyzing historical data, market trends, and customer preferences, companies can estimate future demand and adjust their inventory levels accordingly. This enables them to prevent stockouts and excessive inventory, thus avoiding financial losses and maintaining customer satisfaction.

In conclusion, inventory management is a critical component of supply chain management in industrial engineering. By implementing efficient inventory management strategies, utilizing advanced technologies, and accurately forecasting demand, companies can optimize their operations, reduce costs, and enhance customer satisfaction. Successful inventory management is key to delivering success in the dynamic and competitive business environment.

Warehousing and Distribution

In today's fast-paced and highly competitive business environment, effective supply chain management is crucial for the success of any organization. One of the key components of a well-functioning supply chain is the efficient management of warehousing and distribution operations. This subchapter will delve into the importance of warehousing and distribution in the overall supply chain management process and how it contributes to delivering success.

Warehousing serves as a vital link between the production process and the final delivery of goods to the end customer. It provides a centralized location for storing and managing inventory, ensuring that products are readily available when needed. The primary goal of effective warehousing is to minimize costs while maintaining optimal levels of inventory. This is achieved through careful planning, organization, and control of warehouse operations.

Distribution, on the other hand, focuses on the movement of goods from the warehouse to the customer's doorstep. It involves the coordination of transportation, order processing, and delivery to ensure that products reach the right place at the right time. Efficient distribution plays a pivotal role in customer satisfaction, as it ensures timely delivery and reduces the risk of stockouts or delays.

Industrial engineering professionals play a critical role in optimizing warehousing and distribution processes. They utilize various tools and techniques to streamline operations, improve efficiency, and reduce costs. This includes analyzing warehouse layout and design, implementing technology-driven solutions such as warehouse management systems, and optimizing transportation routes for effective distribution.

Efficient warehousing and distribution can provide several benefits to organizations. Firstly, it enables companies to meet customer demands promptly and accurately, thereby enhancing customer satisfaction and loyalty. Secondly, it helps in reducing overall inventory holding costs by ensuring efficient space utilization and minimizing stockouts. Thirdly, it allows companies to respond quickly to market fluctuations and changing customer preferences.

In conclusion, warehousing and distribution are integral components of effective supply chain management. They play a significant role in ensuring the smooth flow of goods from production to the end customer. Industrial engineering professionals have a crucial role to play in optimizing these processes to achieve maximum efficiency and cost-effectiveness. By focusing on continuous improvement and leveraging technology, organizations can harness the power of effective warehousing and distribution to deliver success in today's competitive business landscape.

Transportation and Logistics

Transportation and logistics play a crucial role in the success of any supply chain management system. This subchapter aims to provide a comprehensive overview of the importance of transportation and logistics in the field of industrial engineering. Whether you are a student, professional, or simply curious about the subject, this content will equip you with the necessary knowledge to understand and appreciate the power of effective transportation and logistics.

Transportation refers to the movement of goods or people from one location to another. In the context of supply chain management, it involves the physical movement of products from suppliers to manufacturers, from manufacturers to distributors, and ultimately to the end consumers. The choice of transportation mode, such as road, rail, air, or sea, depends on factors like cost, speed, and nature of the goods being transported.

Logistics, on the other hand, encompasses the entire process of planning, implementing, and controlling the efficient and effective flow of goods and services. It involves activities such as inventory management, warehousing, packaging, and order fulfillment. Logistics aims to ensure that the right product is delivered to the right place, at the right time, and in the right condition.

Effective transportation and logistics have a significant impact on the overall supply chain performance. It can enhance customer satisfaction by ensuring timely delivery and reducing stockouts. Efficient transportation and logistics systems also result in cost savings, improved productivity, and increased profitability for organizations.

In this subchapter, we will explore various aspects of transportation and logistics, including different modes of transportation, key considerations in logistics planning, and emerging trends in the field. We will also delve into the role of technology, such as transportation management systems and real-time tracking, in optimizing transportation and logistics operations.

Whether you are a student studying industrial engineering or a professional seeking to enhance your understanding of transportation and logistics, this subchapter will provide valuable insights into the power of effective supply chain management. By the end, you will have a solid foundation to appreciate and contribute to the transportation and logistics aspects of any supply chain management system.

Demand Planning and Forecasting

In the dynamic world of supply chain management, demand planning and forecasting play a crucial role in enabling organizations to meet customer demands effectively. This subchapter explores the significance of demand planning and forecasting in the context of industrial engineering, providing valuable insights and best practices to ensure success in supply chain management.

Demand planning is the process of estimating future customer demand for a product or service. By analyzing historical data, market trends, and customer preferences, organizations can accurately forecast demand and make informed decisions related to production, inventory management, and resource allocation. Industrial engineers, with their expertise in optimizing processes and systems, have a vital role to play in this process.

Effective demand planning is essential for industrial engineering as it helps organizations minimize stockouts, reduce excess inventory, and enhance customer satisfaction. By accurately predicting demand, industrial engineers can optimize production schedules, streamline operations, and improve overall supply chain efficiency. This ultimately leads to cost savings and increased profitability for organizations.

In this subchapter, we delve into the various techniques and methodologies used in demand planning and forecasting. We explore the importance of data analysis, statistical modeling, and collaboration across departments to ensure accurate demand forecasts. We also discuss the challenges faced in demand planning, such as demand volatility, seasonality, and market uncertainties, and provide strategies to mitigate these challenges.

Furthermore, we highlight the role of technology and automation in demand planning and forecasting. Industrial engineers can leverage advanced software solutions, artificial intelligence, and machine learning algorithms to improve forecast accuracy and enable real-time demand sensing. We also emphasize the importance of continuous improvement and the need to regularly reassess and adjust demand plans based on changing market conditions.

This subchapter aims to equip industrial engineers with the knowledge and skills required to excel in demand planning and forecasting. By understanding the intricacies of demand forecasting, industrial engineers can contribute significantly to supply chain optimization and drive organizational success.

Whether you are an industrial engineering professional or someone interested in supply chain management, this subchapter provides valuable insights and practical tips to enhance your understanding of demand planning and forecasting. By mastering these concepts, you can play a pivotal role in delivering success through effective supply chain management.

Chapter 3: Strategies for Effective Supply Chain Management

Lean Supply Chain Management

In today's competitive business landscape, it is crucial for organizations to continuously improve their supply chain management practices in order to stay ahead. One such approach that has gained significant traction is Lean Supply Chain Management. This subchapter will explore the concept of Lean Supply Chain Management and its benefits, with a focus on the industrial engineering niche.

Lean Supply Chain Management is a philosophy that aims to eliminate waste and maximize value creation at every stage of the supply chain. It draws inspiration from the principles of Lean Manufacturing, which originated from the Toyota Production System. By applying Lean principles to the entire supply chain, organizations can achieve operational excellence, improve customer satisfaction, and increase profitability.

One of the core principles of Lean Supply Chain Management is the elimination of waste. This involves identifying and eliminating non-value-added activities, such as excessive inventory, overproduction, transportation inefficiencies, and unnecessary processing steps. By streamlining processes and reducing waste, organizations can achieve cost savings, shorten lead times, and enhance overall efficiency.

Another key aspect of Lean Supply Chain Management is the focus on continuous improvement. Organizations are encouraged to embrace a culture of continuous learning and innovation, constantly seeking opportunities for improvement. This involves empowering employees to identify and solve problems, fostering collaboration with suppliers and customers, and leveraging technology to optimize processes.

In the industrial engineering niche, Lean Supply Chain Management offers significant benefits. By implementing Lean practices, organizations can optimize their manufacturing processes, reduce production lead times, and improve product quality. This can result in increased productivity, reduced costs, and enhanced customer satisfaction. Furthermore, Lean Supply Chain Management enables organizations to build strong relationships with suppliers, ensuring a reliable and efficient flow of materials.

In conclusion, Lean Supply Chain Management is a powerful approach that can help organizations in the industrial engineering niche achieve operational excellence and gain a competitive edge. By eliminating waste, fostering continuous improvement, and building strong relationships with suppliers, organizations can optimize their supply chain processes and deliver superior value to customers. Embracing the principles of Lean Supply Chain Management is essential in today's fast-paced and ever-changing business environment.

Agile Supply Chain Management

In today's fast-paced and ever-changing business landscape, companies must adapt and respond quickly to market demands to stay competitive. This is especially true for the industrial engineering sector, where efficient supply chain management is crucial for delivering success. In this subchapter, we will explore the concept of Agile Supply Chain Management and its importance in the industrial engineering niche.

Agile Supply Chain Management refers to the ability of a company to quickly and effectively respond to unforeseen changes and disruptions in the supply chain. It emphasizes flexibility, adaptability, and responsiveness, enabling organizations to rapidly adjust their operations to meet customer demands and market fluctuations. This approach is particularly relevant in the industrial engineering field, where projects often involve complex processes and multiple stakeholders.

One of the key aspects of Agile Supply Chain Management is collaboration. Effective communication and collaboration among various departments, suppliers, and customers are essential for ensuring a smooth flow of materials and information. By fostering strong relationships and leveraging technology, industrial engineering firms can enhance their supply chain visibility and transparency, reducing delays and improving overall efficiency.

Another crucial element of Agile Supply Chain Management is the use of real-time data and analytics. By leveraging advanced technologies such as Internet of Things (IoT), artificial intelligence (AI), and big data analytics, companies can gain valuable insights into their supply chain operations. This enables them to identify potential bottlenecks, predict disruptions, and proactively address issues before they escalate. Such data-driven decision-making can significantly enhance operational efficiency, reduce costs, and improve customer satisfaction.

Additionally, Agile Supply Chain Management encourages companies to embrace continuous improvement and innovation. By constantly seeking ways to optimize processes, eliminate waste, and enhance product quality, industrial engineering firms can stay ahead of the competition and deliver superior value to their customers. This can be achieved through the adoption of lean manufacturing principles, just-in-time inventory management, and cross-functional teams focused on innovation.

Overall, Agile Supply Chain Management is a critical concept for the industrial engineering niche. It enables organizations to navigate the ever-changing business landscape with agility and resilience, effectively meeting customer demands and maintaining a competitive edge. By embracing collaboration, leveraging technology, and fostering continuous improvement, companies can enhance their supply chain efficiency, reduce costs, and ultimately deliver success in the industrial engineering sector.

Just-in-Time (JIT) Supply Chain Management

In today's fast-paced and highly competitive business environment, supply chain management plays a critical role in the success of any organization. One highly effective approach to managing the supply chain is Just-in-Time (JIT) Supply Chain Management. This subchapter will delve into the concept of JIT and its significance in industrial engineering.

JIT is a philosophy that emphasizes the elimination of waste by delivering the right quantity of products or materials at the right time and place. The primary objective of JIT is to minimize inventory levels while maximizing efficiency and reducing costs. By adopting a JIT approach, organizations can ensure that they receive materials exactly when they are needed, eliminating the need for excessive inventory and associated storage costs.

In the context of industrial engineering, JIT Supply Chain Management can revolutionize the way businesses operate. By streamlining the supply chain, organizations can enhance their production processes, reduce lead times, and increase customer satisfaction. Industrial engineers are essential in implementing JIT principles as they are equipped with the skills to analyze and optimize complex systems.

Implementing JIT requires a high level of coordination and collaboration among all stakeholders involved in the supply chain. Effective communication and information sharing are crucial to ensure that each party understands their role and responsibilities. Suppliers need to align their production schedules with the demand patterns of the organization, while customers must provide accurate forecasts to allow suppliers to plan and deliver accordingly.

JIT Supply Chain Management also relies heavily on the use of technology and automation. Advanced software systems can provide real-time visibility into inventory levels, production schedules, and customer demand. This enables organizations to make data-driven decisions and respond quickly to changes in the market. Industrial engineers are instrumental in selecting and implementing these technological solutions, ensuring seamless integration and optimization.

Furthermore, JIT Supply Chain Management promotes continuous improvement and lean manufacturing principles. Organizations must constantly strive to identify and eliminate bottlenecks, reduce waste, and enhance overall efficiency. Industrial engineers play a pivotal role in conducting time studies, analyzing production processes, and implementing improvements to maximize productivity.

In conclusion, Just-in-Time (JIT) Supply Chain Management is a powerful approach that can significantly benefit organizations in the industrial engineering sector. By eliminating waste, optimizing inventory levels, and fostering collaboration, organizations can achieve higher efficiency, reduced costs, and increased customer satisfaction. Industrial engineers are instrumental in implementing JIT principles and leveraging technology to streamline the supply chain and drive success.

Efficient Consumer Response (ECR)

In today's fast-paced and highly competitive business environment, supply chain management has become a critical factor for success. One of the key strategies that organizations can adopt to enhance their supply chain efficiency is Efficient Consumer Response (ECR). This subchapter aims to provide a comprehensive overview of ECR and its benefits for industrial engineering professionals and a broader audience.

Efficient Consumer Response is a collaborative approach that focuses on meeting consumer demands by optimizing the entire supply chain. It involves the integration of various stakeholders, including manufacturers, retailers, and suppliers, to streamline processes, reduce costs, and improve customer satisfaction. ECR aims to minimize waste, improve inventory management, and enhance communication and coordination among all parties involved in the supply chain.

For industrial engineering professionals, ECR offers a multitude of benefits. By adopting ECR principles, organizations can optimize their production processes, reduce lead times, and improve overall efficiency. This not only leads to cost savings but also enables faster response times to changing market demands. Industrial engineers can leverage their expertise to identify bottlenecks, streamline operations, and implement innovative technologies to enhance the effectiveness of ECR initiatives.

For everyone interested in supply chain management, understanding ECR is crucial as it revolutionizes the way products are delivered to consumers. ECR emphasizes the importance of collaboration and information sharing throughout the supply chain, enabling organizations to respond more effectively to consumer needs. By adopting ECR practices, companies can reduce stockouts, improve product availability, and enhance customer satisfaction.

In addition to its benefits for industrial engineering professionals and the broader audience, ECR also has a significant impact on sustainability. By optimizing the supply chain and reducing waste, ECR contributes to a more environmentally friendly approach to business. This is particularly relevant in today's world, where consumers are increasingly conscious of the ecological impact of their purchasing decisions.

In conclusion, Efficient Consumer Response (ECR) is a powerful strategy that can revolutionize supply chain management. By adopting ECR principles, organizations can enhance efficiency, reduce costs, and improve customer satisfaction. Industrial engineering professionals can leverage their skills to optimize ECR initiatives and drive meaningful improvements in supply chain operations. For everyone interested in supply chain management, understanding ECR is essential to stay competitive in today's dynamic business landscape.

Vendor-Managed Inventory (VMI)

In today's highly competitive business environment, effective supply chain management has become crucial for organizations across various industries. One of the key strategies that can help organizations streamline their supply chain processes is Vendor-Managed Inventory (VMI).

VMI is a collaborative approach between suppliers and their customers, particularly in the industrial engineering niche. It involves the supplier taking responsibility for managing the inventory levels of their products at the customer's location. This approach allows businesses to optimize their inventory levels, reduce costs, and improve overall supply chain efficiency.

In traditional inventory management systems, customers are responsible for forecasting and placing orders for the products they need. However, this approach often leads to inventory imbalances, stockouts, and excess inventory, resulting in increased costs and reduced customer satisfaction. VMI seeks to address these challenges by enabling suppliers to take control of inventory management, ensuring that the right products are available at the right time and in the right quantities.

By implementing VMI, organizations in the industrial engineering niche can experience several benefits. Firstly, it eliminates the need for customers to invest in large amounts of inventory, freeing up valuable resources that can be allocated to other business areas. This helps to reduce carrying costs and improve cash flow.

Secondly, VMI enables suppliers to have real-time visibility into customer demand, allowing them to plan production and manage inventory more effectively. This can lead to improved order fulfillment rates, reduced lead times, and increased customer satisfaction, ultimately enhancing the competitive advantage of both the supplier and the customer.

Moreover, VMI fosters closer collaboration and communication between suppliers and customers. By sharing information and working together to optimize inventory levels, both parties can align their goals and objectives, resulting in a more efficient and responsive supply chain.

In conclusion, Vendor-Managed Inventory (VMI) is a powerful tool that can transform supply chain management in the industrial engineering niche. By allowing suppliers to take control of inventory management, organizations can optimize inventory levels, reduce costs, and improve overall supply chain efficiency. With its numerous benefits, VMI has the potential to deliver success to businesses across industries by streamlining their supply chain processes and enhancing customer satisfaction.

Chapter 4: Technology and Automation in Supply Chain Management

Role of Technology in Supply Chain Management

In today's rapidly evolving business landscape, the role of technology in supply chain management has become increasingly critical. With the advent of advanced technologies, such as artificial intelligence, blockchain, and the Internet of Things (IoT), industrial engineering professionals have been able to revolutionize supply chain operations, enhancing efficiency, transparency, and overall business performance.

One of the key benefits of technology in supply chain management is improved visibility. Through the use of sophisticated software systems, companies can now track their inventory in real-time, ensuring accurate and up-to-date information on product availability and location. This visibility enables industrial engineers to make informed decisions regarding inventory management, demand forecasting, and order fulfillment, ultimately reducing stockouts and minimizing carrying costs.

Moreover, technology plays a significant role in streamlining communication and collaboration within the supply chain network. With the help of cloud-based platforms and digital communication tools, industrial engineers can easily share information and collaborate with suppliers, manufacturers, and distributors. This seamless flow of data and communication ensures that all stakeholders are on the same page, enabling faster response times, better coordination, and improved customer satisfaction.

Furthermore, technology has enabled the automation of various supply chain processes, reducing the reliance on manual labor and minimizing the risk of human error. Industrial engineers can now leverage automated systems for tasks such as order processing, inventory replenishment, and transportation management. This automation not only improves accuracy and efficiency but also frees up valuable time for engineers to focus on strategic decision-making and continuous process improvement.

In addition to automation, technology has also paved the way for predictive analytics in supply chain management. By analyzing vast amounts of data collected from various sources, industrial engineers can now forecast demand patterns, identify potential bottlenecks, and optimize supply chain operations. This predictive capability empowers companies to make proactive decisions, avoid disruptions, and optimize their resources for maximum efficiency and cost-effectiveness.

Overall, the role of technology in supply chain management cannot be overstated. It has become a driving force behind successful supply chain operations, enabling industrial engineers to overcome challenges and deliver superior performance. By leveraging advanced technologies, companies can enhance visibility, streamline communication, automate processes, and leverage predictive analytics, ultimately achieving a competitive edge in today's dynamic business environment.

Supply Chain Management Software and Tools

In today's fast-paced and highly competitive business environment, effective supply chain management is crucial for the success of any organization. To streamline and optimize their supply chain processes, industrial engineering professionals need to leverage advanced software and tools specifically designed for supply chain management.

Supply chain management software provides a comprehensive solution to manage and coordinate the flow of goods, information, and finances from the point of origin to the point of consumption. These software solutions enable organizations to enhance their operational efficiency, reduce costs, and improve customer satisfaction. With the increasing complexity of global supply chains, the use of such software has become indispensable.

One of the key advantages of supply chain management software is its ability to automate various processes, including inventory management, demand forecasting, order processing, and logistics coordination. By automating these tasks, industrial engineers can save valuable time and focus on strategic decision-making. Moreover, the software allows for real-time visibility into the entire supply chain, enabling proactive problem-solving and better decision-making.

Supply chain management tools complement the software by providing additional functionalities and capabilities. These tools can vary from simple spreadsheet-based templates to sophisticated analytics platforms. Some of the common tools used in supply chain management include:

1. Demand planning tools: These tools help industrial engineers forecast future demand accurately. By analyzing historical data,

market trends, and other relevant factors, demand planning tools enable organizations to optimize their inventory levels and avoid stock-outs or excess inventory.

2. Transportation management systems: These tools assist in managing the transportation of goods from suppliers to customers. They optimize route planning, load consolidation, and carrier selection, resulting in reduced transportation costs and improved delivery performance.

3. Warehouse management systems: These tools help in efficiently managing warehouse operations, including inventory tracking, order fulfillment, and picking and packing. They ensure that the right products are available at the right time, minimizing stockouts and improving overall warehouse productivity.

4. Supplier relationship management tools: These tools facilitate effective communication and collaboration with suppliers. They help in managing supplier performance, monitoring supplier quality, and tracking supplier deliveries, ensuring a smooth and reliable supply chain.

By leveraging supply chain management software and tools, industrial engineering professionals can gain a competitive edge in the market. These technologies enable them to optimize their supply chain processes, reduce costs, enhance customer satisfaction, and respond quickly to changing market dynamics. As supply chains continue to evolve and become more complex, the use of advanced software and tools becomes increasingly essential for delivering success in supply chain management.

Internet of Things (IoT) in Supply Chain Management

The advent of the Internet of Things (IoT) has revolutionized various industries, and supply chain management is no exception. In this subchapter, we will explore how IoT is transforming the field of supply chain management and revolutionizing the way businesses operate. Whether you are a supply chain professional, an industrial engineer, or simply curious about the latest advancements in technology, this subchapter will provide valuable insights into the power of IoT in the supply chain.

IoT refers to a system of interconnected devices that can communicate and share data with each other through the internet. In the context of supply chain management, IoT enables a seamless exchange of information between various components of the supply chain, such as suppliers, manufacturers, distributors, and customers. This real-time data sharing empowers businesses to make informed decisions, optimize operations, and minimize costs.

One of the key areas where IoT has made a significant impact is inventory management. Through IoT-enabled sensors, businesses can track the movement and location of goods throughout the supply chain. This real-time visibility allows for accurate demand forecasting, efficient inventory management, and reduced stockouts. With IoT, businesses can automate inventory replenishment, ensuring that the right products are available at the right time, thus improving customer satisfaction and minimizing lost sales opportunities.

Furthermore, IoT enables predictive maintenance by monitoring the condition and performance of machinery and equipment in real-time. This proactive approach to maintenance reduces downtime, prevents costly breakdowns, and extends the lifespan of assets. Industrial engineers can leverage IoT data to optimize production processes, identify bottlenecks, and improve overall efficiency.

In addition to inventory management and maintenance, IoT also plays a crucial role in enhancing supply chain visibility and traceability. By integrating IoT devices with transportation systems, businesses can track the movement of goods in real-time, monitor temperature and humidity conditions, and ensure compliance with regulatory standards. This level of transparency not only improves supply chain efficiency but also helps in identifying and addressing potential bottlenecks or disruptions before they escalate.

In conclusion, IoT is revolutionizing supply chain management and transforming the way businesses operate. Industrial engineers, supply chain professionals, and anyone interested in the field can benefit from understanding the power of IoT in optimizing inventory management, enabling predictive maintenance, and enhancing supply chain visibility. Embracing IoT technologies can help businesses unlock new levels of efficiency, reduce costs, and deliver exceptional customer experiences.

Robotics and Automation in Supply Chain Processes

In today's fast-paced and globalized world, supply chain management has become a crucial aspect of any successful business. To ensure efficiency and competitiveness, companies across various industries are turning to robotics and automation to streamline their supply chain processes. This subchapter explores the transformative power of robotics and automation in the field of supply chain management, particularly from the perspective of industrial engineering.

Industrial engineering, as a niche within the broader field of engineering, focuses on optimizing complex systems to enhance productivity and cost-effectiveness. With the advent of robotics and automation, industrial engineers now have a powerful tool at their disposal to revolutionize supply chain processes. By integrating robotics and automation into various stages of the supply chain, companies can achieve higher levels of efficiency, accuracy, and agility.

One major area where robotics and automation have made a significant impact is in warehousing and distribution. Traditionally, these operations involved manual labor, which was time-consuming, error-prone, and often inefficient. However, with the introduction of automated guided vehicles (AGVs) and robotic systems, companies can now automate tasks such as picking, packing, and sorting, resulting in faster order fulfillment and reduced errors.

Furthermore, robotics and automation have also enabled the implementation of advanced inventory management systems. With the help of sensors, RFID tags, and data analytics, companies can track and monitor inventory levels in real-time, ensuring optimal stock levels and reducing the risk of stockouts or overstocking. This level of automation allows for improved demand forecasting, efficient replenishment, and seamless integration with suppliers and customers.

Another area where robotics and automation have proven invaluable is in transportation and logistics. Automated vehicles and drones are increasingly being used to transport goods, reducing human error and improving delivery speed. Additionally, predictive analytics and machine learning algorithms are employed to optimize routes and minimize fuel consumption, resulting in cost savings and reduced carbon emissions.

In conclusion, robotics and automation have revolutionized supply chain processes, offering significant benefits to companies in terms of efficiency, accuracy, and cost-effectiveness. Industrial engineers play a vital role in harnessing the power of robotics and automation, ensuring the seamless integration of these technologies into supply chain management. By embracing robotics and automation, businesses can gain a competitive edge in today's rapidly evolving markets, while industrial engineers continue to drive innovation and efficiency in the field of supply chain management.

Chapter 5: Key Performance Indicators (KPIs) in Supply Chain Management

Importance of KPIs in Measuring Supply Chain Performance

Title: Importance of KPIs in Measuring Supply Chain Performance

Introduction:
In today's rapidly evolving business landscape, effective supply chain management has become a key driver of success across industries. To ensure smooth operations, industrial engineering professionals must understand the significance of key performance indicators (KPIs) in measuring supply chain performance. This subchapter aims to shed light on the importance of KPIs and their role in enhancing overall supply chain efficiency and effectiveness.

Enhancing Visibility and Transparency:
KPIs provide a clear and comprehensive view of various aspects of the supply chain, allowing industrial engineers to identify bottlenecks, inefficiencies, and areas of improvement. By tracking and analyzing KPIs such as inventory turnover, on-time delivery, and order fulfillment rates, professionals gain valuable insights into the performance at different stages of the supply chain. This visibility enables them to make informed decisions and optimize processes, ultimately leading to improved customer satisfaction and reduced costs.

Driving Continuous Improvement:
KPIs act as a benchmark against which supply chain performance can be measured over time. By establishing quantifiable targets and regularly monitoring KPIs, industrial engineers can identify trends, set

goals, and drive continuous improvement initiatives. Performance metrics such as supplier lead time, cycle time, and order accuracy provide vital information to assess process efficiency and identify areas for optimization. This data-driven approach fosters a culture of continuous improvement, enabling organizations to stay ahead of the competition.

Aligning Supply Chain with Business Objectives: KPIs play a crucial role in aligning supply chain activities with broader business objectives. By selecting relevant metrics that reflect the organization's goals, industrial engineers ensure that the supply chain operates in sync with strategic priorities. Whether it's reducing costs, increasing customer satisfaction, or improving sustainability, well-defined KPIs help measure progress and ensure that the supply chain supports the overall business strategy.

Facilitating Collaboration and Communication: Supply chains involve multiple stakeholders and departments, making effective collaboration and communication vital for success. KPIs provide a common language and framework for discussions between different teams, fostering collaboration and enhancing understanding. By sharing and analyzing KPI data, industrial engineers can identify interdependencies, streamline processes, and align goals, resulting in improved coordination and overall supply chain performance.

Conclusion:

In today's complex and competitive business environment, the importance of KPIs in measuring supply chain performance cannot be overstated. Industrial engineering professionals must recognize the power of KPIs in enhancing visibility, driving continuous improvement, aligning activities with business objectives, and facilitating collaboration. By leveraging KPIs effectively, organizations can optimize their supply chains, deliver superior performance, and achieve long-term success.

Commonly Used KPIs in Supply Chain Management

In the fast-paced world of supply chain management, it is crucial to have a set of key performance indicators (KPIs) to effectively measure and monitor the performance of your supply chain processes. These KPIs provide valuable insights into the efficiency, productivity, and overall effectiveness of your supply chain operations. In this subchapter, we will explore some commonly used KPIs in supply chain management that can help you deliver success in your operations.

1. On-time Delivery: A critical KPI in supply chain management, on-time delivery measures the percentage of orders delivered to customers within the agreed-upon time frame. This KPI helps assess the reliability of your supply chain in meeting customer expectations and avoiding disruptions.

2. Order Accuracy: This KPI measures the percentage of orders that are fulfilled accurately without any errors or discrepancies. Maintaining high order accuracy ensures customer satisfaction, minimizes returns, and reduces costs associated with rework or replacements.

3. Inventory Turnover: Inventory turnover is a KPI that evaluates how quickly your inventory is being sold and replenished. It measures the number of times inventory is sold and replaced within a specific time period. A high turnover rate indicates efficient inventory management, while a low rate may suggest excess inventory or slow sales.

4. Fill Rate: Fill rate measures the percentage of customer orders that are completely fulfilled from available inventory. It reflects the ability

of your supply chain to meet customer demand promptly. A high fill rate indicates a well-managed supply chain with minimal stockouts and backorders.

5. Supplier Performance: This KPI assesses the performance of your suppliers, including factors such as on-time delivery, quality of goods or services, and responsiveness. Monitoring supplier performance helps identify potential bottlenecks or risks in your supply chain and enables you to take proactive measures.

6. Transportation Cost: This KPI measures the cost of transportation per unit or per shipment. It helps evaluate the efficiency and cost-effectiveness of your transportation operations. By monitoring transportation costs, you can identify opportunities for optimization and cost reduction.

7. Perfect Order Rate: Perfect order rate measures the percentage of orders that are delivered on time, in full, and without any errors. It combines multiple aspects of supply chain performance into a single metric and provides a holistic view of overall operational effectiveness.

These are just a few examples of commonly used KPIs in supply chain management. By tracking and analyzing these metrics, you can gain valuable insights into your supply chain operations, identify areas for improvement, and make data-driven decisions to enhance efficiency, reduce costs, and ultimately deliver success in your industrial engineering endeavors.

Setting and Tracking KPIs for Supply Chain Success

In the world of supply chain management, success is often determined by the ability to effectively set and track key performance indicators (KPIs). These metrics provide valuable insights into the performance of various aspects of the supply chain, helping organizations identify areas for improvement and make data-driven decisions. This subchapter will delve into the importance of setting and tracking KPIs for achieving supply chain success and how they can benefit professionals in the field of industrial engineering.

Setting KPIs is crucial because it allows organizations to define and measure their desired outcomes. By establishing clear goals and objectives, companies can align their supply chain activities with overarching business strategies. Whether it is reducing costs, improving delivery times, or enhancing customer satisfaction, KPIs provide a roadmap for success. Industrial engineers, who are responsible for optimizing processes and systems, can utilize KPIs to identify bottlenecks and implement improvements that will positively impact the entire supply chain.

Tracking KPIs is equally important as it enables organizations to monitor their progress and evaluate performance. By regularly measuring and analyzing KPI data, industrial engineers can identify trends, patterns, and areas of concern. For example, if a KPI related to on-time delivery deteriorates, it could indicate issues with transportation or warehouse operations. Armed with this information, industrial engineers can take immediate corrective actions, such as optimizing routes or streamlining warehouse layouts, to ensure timely deliveries and maintain customer satisfaction.

The benefits of setting and tracking KPIs extend beyond problem-solving and optimization. They also foster a culture of continuous improvement within supply chain organizations. By regularly reviewing and discussing KPI data, teams can collaborate and brainstorm innovative solutions. Industrial engineers can leverage KPIs to initiate projects aimed at process improvement, cost reduction, and enhanced customer experiences. This not only boosts operational efficiency but also promotes employee engagement and drives overall supply chain success.

In conclusion, setting and tracking KPIs are essential for achieving supply chain success in the field of industrial engineering. These metrics provide a framework for organizations to define objectives, align activities, and monitor performance. By leveraging KPIs, industrial engineers can identify areas for improvement, optimize processes, and drive continuous improvement. Whether you are a supply chain professional or an industrial engineer, understanding the power of setting and tracking KPIs is crucial for delivering success in today's competitive business landscape.

Chapter 6: Supply Chain Risk Management

Identifying and Assessing Supply Chain Risks

In the fast-paced and ever-evolving world of supply chain management, it is crucial for professionals in the field of industrial engineering to understand and effectively manage risks that can potentially disrupt their operations. The ability to identify and assess supply chain risks is essential for success in this industry, as it allows for proactive measures to be put in place, mitigating the impact of potential disruptions and ensuring the smooth flow of goods and services.

The first step in identifying and assessing supply chain risks is to develop a comprehensive understanding of the entire supply chain network. This involves mapping out all the processes, activities, and entities involved in delivering a product or service to the end customer. By doing so, it becomes easier to identify potential points of failure or vulnerabilities that could lead to disruptions.

Once the supply chain network has been mapped out, the next step is to identify the various risks that could impact the smooth functioning of the supply chain. These risks can come in various forms, such as natural disasters, political instability, supplier bankruptcy, or even cyber-attacks. It is important to conduct a thorough analysis of each risk, considering its likelihood of occurrence and the potential impact it could have on the supply chain.

After the risks have been identified, they need to be assessed in terms of their severity and potential consequences. This involves quantifying the risks based on their likelihood and impact, and ranking them in order of priority. By doing so, industrial engineering professionals can focus their efforts on addressing the most critical risks first, ensuring that the necessary resources and strategies are put in place to mitigate their impact.

In addition to identifying and assessing risks, it is also important to continuously monitor the supply chain for any new or emerging risks. The business environment is constantly changing, and new risks can arise unexpectedly. By staying vigilant and keeping an eye on industry trends and developments, industrial engineering professionals can proactively respond to potential risks and minimize their impact on the supply chain.

In conclusion, identifying and assessing supply chain risks is a critical component of effective supply chain management for industrial engineering professionals. By mapping out the supply chain network, identifying potential risks, and assessing their severity, professionals can proactively mitigate the impact of disruptions and ensure the smooth flow of goods and services. Continuous monitoring and adaptation are also crucial to stay ahead of new and emerging risks. By implementing these strategies, industrial engineering professionals can deliver success in their supply chain operations.

Strategies for Mitigating Supply Chain Risks

In today's rapidly evolving business landscape, supply chain management has become a critical component for success. With increasing globalization, technological advancements, and economic uncertainties, industrial engineering professionals must be equipped with strategies to effectively mitigate supply chain risks. This subchapter aims to provide valuable insights and practical approaches for managing and minimizing these risks.

1. Diversification of Suppliers: Relying on a single supplier can expose businesses to significant risks. By diversifying the supplier base, industrial engineers can ensure continuity of operations even in the face of unforeseen disruptions. This strategy involves identifying and qualifying alternative suppliers, fostering relationships, and distributing orders among them.

2. Demand Forecasting and Planning: Accurate demand forecasting is crucial for optimizing supply chain operations. Industrial engineers should leverage data analytics, market research, and historical trends to forecast demand patterns accurately. By aligning production and inventory levels with anticipated demand, businesses can reduce the risk of overstocking or stockouts.

3. Inventory Management: Effective inventory management is a cornerstone of supply chain risk mitigation. Industrial engineers should adopt just-in-time (JIT) or lean inventory management techniques to minimize holding costs while ensuring product availability. By monitoring inventory levels in real-time, businesses can respond promptly to demand fluctuations and avoid excess inventory or shortages.

4. Supplier Relationship Management: Strong relationships with suppliers are essential for managing supply chain risks. Industrial engineers should establish open lines of communication, foster collaboration, and conduct regular performance evaluations. By maintaining transparency and trust, businesses can address potential issues proactively and work together to find solutions.

5. Supply Chain Visibility: Enhancing visibility across the supply chain is crucial for identifying and mitigating risks promptly. Industrial engineers should leverage advanced technologies such as blockchain, Internet of Things (IoT), and cloud computing to gain real-time insights into the movement of goods. This enables better risk assessment, early identification of bottlenecks, and faster response to disruptions.

6. Scenario Planning and Contingency Strategies: Industrial engineers should develop contingency plans and conduct scenario planning exercises to prepare for potential disruptions. By anticipating various risk scenarios, businesses can identify critical vulnerabilities, develop alternative strategies, and minimize the impact of disruptions on the supply chain.

In conclusion, effective supply chain management is essential for businesses across all industries. Industrial engineers play a crucial role in mitigating supply chain risks by adopting strategies such as supplier diversification, demand forecasting, inventory management, supplier relationship management, enhancing supply chain visibility, and developing contingency plans. By implementing these strategies, businesses can enhance their resilience, optimize operations, and deliver consistent success in an increasingly uncertain business environment.

Building Resilience in the Supply Chain

In today's rapidly changing and uncertain business environment, building resilience in the supply chain has become more crucial than ever before. The ability to effectively manage disruptions and adapt to unexpected challenges is vital for the success of any organization, particularly in the field of industrial engineering. This subchapter will explore the concept of resilience in the supply chain and provide valuable insights on how to enhance it.

Resilience can be defined as the capacity to withstand, adapt, and recover from disruptions while maintaining continuous operations. It requires a proactive approach that considers potential risks and incorporates strategies to mitigate their impact. With the increasing complexity of supply chains and the interconnectedness of global markets, organizations must be prepared to tackle various potential disruptions, such as natural disasters, political instability, supplier failures, and demand fluctuations.

One key aspect of building resilience in the supply chain is having a robust risk management strategy. This involves identifying potential risks, assessing their likelihood and impact, and developing contingency plans to mitigate them. By conducting thorough risk assessments and implementing measures like dual sourcing, safety stock, and alternate transportation routes, organizations can enhance their ability to respond effectively to unexpected events.

Another crucial factor in building resilience is establishing strong relationships with suppliers and partners. Collaboration and communication are essential for sharing information, coordinating efforts, and developing joint contingency plans. Regularly engaging with suppliers, conducting audits, and fostering open lines of communication will not only strengthen relationships but also enable organizations to identify potential vulnerabilities and implement necessary improvements.

Furthermore, leveraging technology and data analytics can significantly enhance supply chain resilience. By implementing advanced forecasting tools, real-time tracking systems, and predictive analytics, organizations can gain better visibility into their supply chains. This enables them to detect potential disruptions early on, respond quickly, and make informed decisions to minimize the impact on operations.

Ultimately, building resilience in the supply chain requires a proactive and holistic approach. It necessitates a strong commitment from all stakeholders involved, including top management, suppliers, and partners. By continuously monitoring and assessing the supply chain, identifying potential risks, and implementing robust risk management strategies, organizations can enhance their ability to navigate uncertainty and ensure the uninterrupted flow of goods and services.

In conclusion, resilience in the supply chain is of utmost importance for the industrial engineering sector. By incorporating proactive risk management strategies, fostering strong relationships, and leveraging technology, organizations can build a resilient supply chain capable of withstanding disruptions and ensuring continued success in an ever-changing business landscape.

Crisis Management and Business Continuity Planning

In today's fast-paced and interconnected world, businesses face numerous challenges that can disrupt their operations and threaten their survival. From natural disasters to cyber attacks, the potential crises that organizations can encounter are vast and varied. Therefore, it is crucial for businesses to have a comprehensive crisis management and business continuity plan in place to mitigate risks and ensure their long-term success.

Crisis management involves identifying potential crises, developing strategies to deal with them, and effectively responding when they occur. It is a proactive approach that aims to minimize the impact of a crisis and protect the organization's reputation. By having a crisis management plan, businesses can quickly respond to emergencies, maintain customer trust, and safeguard their employees and assets.

Business continuity planning, on the other hand, focuses on ensuring that critical operations can continue during and after a crisis. It involves identifying essential business functions, establishing backup systems and processes, and creating a framework for recovery. By developing a robust business continuity plan, organizations can minimize downtime, recover quickly, and maintain customer satisfaction.

Industrial engineering plays a vital role in crisis management and business continuity planning. Industrial engineers are trained to analyze complex systems, identify vulnerabilities, and develop efficient processes. Their expertise can be applied to design and implement strategies that enhance a business's ability to handle crises.

In the book "Delivering Success: The Power of Effective Supply Chain Management," we delve into the key principles and best practices of crisis management and business continuity planning. We provide practical insights and case studies that demonstrate how organizations can effectively manage crises and ensure business continuity.

Whether you are a business owner, manager, or industrial engineering professional, this subchapter will equip you with the necessary knowledge and tools to navigate through crises successfully. By understanding the importance of crisis management and business continuity planning, you can safeguard your organization's future and deliver success in the face of adversity.

In conclusion, crisis management and business continuity planning are essential components of effective supply chain management. By implementing these strategies, businesses can protect themselves from various risks, maintain operational stability, and deliver consistent value to their customers. This subchapter provides a comprehensive guide to help individuals and organizations navigate through crises and ensure long-term success in the industrial engineering field.

Chapter 7: Sustainability and Ethical Considerations in Supply Chain Management

Sustainable Supply Chain Management Practices

In today's rapidly changing world, sustainable supply chain management practices have become increasingly vital for businesses across various industries. This subchapter aims to provide a comprehensive understanding of sustainable supply chain management and its importance in the field of industrial engineering.

Sustainable supply chain management refers to the integration of environmentally friendly practices, social responsibility, and economic viability into every stage of the supply chain. It focuses on minimizing the negative impacts on the environment while maximizing efficiency and profitability. This approach recognizes that businesses have a responsibility to not only meet their financial goals but also contribute to the well-being of society and the planet.

Industrial engineering professionals play a crucial role in implementing sustainable supply chain management practices. By optimizing operations, reducing waste, and promoting ethical sourcing, they can create a positive impact on both the environment and the bottom line. These practices include:

1. Green Procurement: Industrial engineers can select suppliers who prioritize sustainable practices, such as using renewable materials and minimizing waste generation. This ensures that the entire supply chain is aligned with sustainability goals.

2. Energy Efficiency: Implementing energy-saving measures, such as using advanced technologies and optimizing transportation routes,

can significantly reduce greenhouse gas emissions and lower operational costs.

3. Waste Reduction: Industrial engineers can implement waste management strategies, such as recycling and reusing materials, to minimize the environmental impact and promote a circular economy.

4. Ethical Labor Practices: Ensuring fair treatment of workers, providing safe working conditions, and promoting diversity and inclusion are crucial aspects of sustainable supply chain management. Industrial engineers can collaborate with human resources departments to assess and address any labor-related issues within the supply chain.

5. Collaboration and Transparency: Building strong partnerships with suppliers, customers, and stakeholders is essential for implementing sustainable supply chain practices. This includes sharing information and collaborating on sustainability initiatives to drive positive change throughout the supply chain.

By adopting sustainable supply chain management practices, businesses can not only reduce their environmental footprint but also enhance their reputation, attract eco-conscious customers, and improve overall operational efficiency. Moreover, these practices contribute to long-term profitability by minimizing risks associated with regulatory compliance and resource scarcity.

In conclusion, sustainable supply chain management practices are crucial for industrial engineering professionals and businesses at large. By incorporating green procurement, energy efficiency, waste reduction, ethical labor practices, and fostering collaboration, they can create a more sustainable future while achieving their financial goals. It is the responsibility of every individual and organization to understand and implement these practices to ensure the well-being of both people and the planet.

Ethical Sourcing and Fair Trade

In today's interconnected world, where supply chains extend across continents and industries, the concept of ethical sourcing and fair trade has gained significant importance. This subchapter aims to shed light on the significance of ethical sourcing and fair trade practices within the context of supply chain management, specifically targeting the audience of industrial engineering professionals. However, the information presented here is relevant to everyone, as it concerns the ethical implications of our consumer choices.

Ethical sourcing refers to the procurement of goods and services in a manner that aligns with moral and social values. It involves the consideration of factors such as labor conditions, environmental impact, and human rights throughout the supply chain. By focusing on ethical sourcing, companies can ensure that their products are not associated with exploitative practices or harm to the environment.

Fair trade, on the other hand, focuses on creating equitable partnerships between producers in developing countries and buyers in developed nations. It aims to provide fair compensation to producers, promote sustainable practices, and empower marginalized communities. Fair trade certifications guarantee that products meet specific social, economic, and environmental standards.

Industrial engineering professionals play a critical role in ensuring ethical sourcing and fair trade practices within their organizations. They are responsible for designing and managing supply chains that prioritize transparency, traceability, and accountability. By evaluating suppliers' practices, conducting audits, and implementing corrective actions, industrial engineers can contribute to a more ethical supply chain.

However, ethical sourcing and fair trade are not limited to the responsibilities of industrial engineers alone. Consumers also have a crucial role to play. By making informed purchasing decisions, individuals can support companies that prioritize ethical sourcing and fair trade practices. This includes choosing products with recognized certifications, such as Fairtrade, Rainforest Alliance, or B Corp, which signify a commitment to ethical production.

Moreover, governments and regulatory bodies must establish and enforce legislation that promotes ethical sourcing and fair trade. By doing so, they create a level playing field for companies, encourage responsible practices, and protect vulnerable stakeholders.

In conclusion, ethical sourcing and fair trade are vital components of effective supply chain management. Industrial engineering professionals, as well as consumers, have a shared responsibility to promote and support ethical practices throughout the supply chain. By doing so, we can create a more sustainable, just, and equitable world.

Corporate Social Responsibility in the Supply Chain

In today's globalized and interconnected world, the concept of Corporate Social Responsibility (CSR) has gained significant importance. It is no longer enough for companies to focus solely on their bottom line; they must also consider the social and environmental impacts of their operations, especially within the supply chain. This subchapter explores the role of CSR in the supply chain and its relevance to the field of industrial engineering.

CSR in the supply chain refers to the efforts made by companies to integrate social and environmental concerns into their sourcing, production, and distribution processes. It goes beyond compliance with legal and regulatory requirements and encompasses a broader commitment to sustainable and ethical practices. By adopting CSR initiatives, companies can contribute to the well-being of society as a whole, while also enhancing their own reputation and brand value.

Industrial engineering plays a crucial role in implementing CSR in the supply chain. Industrial engineers are trained to optimize processes, reduce waste, and improve efficiency. They can apply their expertise to identify areas within the supply chain where CSR practices can be incorporated. For example, they can analyze transportation routes to minimize carbon emissions or suggest alternative suppliers who follow ethical labor practices.

One of the key aspects of CSR in the supply chain is the promotion of fair labor practices. Industrial engineers can help ensure that workers in the supply chain are treated ethically and provided with safe working conditions. They can conduct audits and assessments to identify any potential violations and recommend corrective measures.

By doing so, they contribute to the creation of a more equitable and sustainable supply chain.

Another important aspect of CSR in the supply chain is environmental sustainability. Industrial engineers can analyze processes and identify opportunities to reduce waste, minimize energy consumption, and promote the use of eco-friendly materials. By implementing these changes, companies can reduce their carbon footprint and contribute to the preservation of the environment.

In conclusion, CSR in the supply chain is a vital component of effective supply chain management. It involves integrating social and environmental concerns into sourcing, production, and distribution processes. Industrial engineers have a significant role to play in implementing CSR initiatives within the supply chain. By leveraging their expertise in optimizing processes and improving efficiency, they can contribute to the creation of a more sustainable and socially responsible supply chain. Ultimately, CSR in the supply chain benefits not only the companies involved but also society as a whole.

Environmental Impact and Green Supply Chain Initiatives

In today's rapidly evolving world, the need for sustainable practices and environmental consciousness has become more apparent than ever. Industries across the globe are facing increasing pressure to adopt green initiatives to minimize their environmental impact and contribute to a more sustainable future. This subchapter will delve into the crucial topic of environmental impact and the role of green supply chain initiatives in addressing this pressing issue.

Industrial engineering plays a significant role in shaping supply chain management practices, making it vital for professionals in this field to understand the environmental impact of their operations. By analyzing the entire supply chain, from sourcing raw materials to delivering the final product, industrial engineers can identify potential areas for improvement and develop strategies to minimize environmental harm.

One of the key aspects of green supply chain initiatives is the concept of reducing carbon emissions. Industries are now actively seeking ways to cut down on greenhouse gas emissions by optimizing transportation routes, streamlining logistics operations, and adopting alternative energy sources. Industrial engineers are at the forefront of implementing sustainable practices such as fuel-efficient transportation, electric vehicles, and renewable energy utilization in manufacturing processes.

Furthermore, green supply chain initiatives focus on waste reduction and recycling. Industrial engineers are instrumental in designing efficient production processes that minimize waste generation, implement recycling programs, and promote the use of sustainable materials. By adopting these practices, industries can reduce their ecological footprint and contribute to the circular economy.

In addition to reducing environmental impact, green supply chain initiatives also bring economic benefits. By optimizing processes, minimizing waste, and implementing energy-efficient practices, industries can achieve cost savings in the long run. Moreover, organizations that prioritize sustainability often enjoy enhanced brand reputation and increased customer loyalty, leading to a competitive advantage in the market.

It is crucial for all individuals, regardless of their background or profession, to understand the significance of environmental impact and green supply chain initiatives. By adopting a sustainable mindset, we can collectively work towards preserving our planet for future generations. Whether you are an industrial engineer, a business owner, or a concerned citizen, embracing green supply chain initiatives can make a tangible difference in reducing our environmental footprint and shaping a more sustainable future.

In conclusion, this subchapter has shed light on the importance of addressing environmental impact through green supply chain initiatives. Industrial engineers play a critical role in implementing sustainable practices, optimizing processes, and reducing waste. By adopting green supply chain initiatives, industries can not only minimize their ecological footprint but also enjoy economic benefits and improved brand reputation. It is crucial for everyone, especially those in the field of industrial engineering, to understand and actively participate in creating a more sustainable future.

Chapter 8: Collaboration and Integration in Supply Chain Management

Importance of Collaboration in Supply Chain Management

In today's globalized and interconnected world, collaboration has become an essential component of effective supply chain management. No longer can organizations operate in isolation; instead, they must foster collaboration and synergy among various stakeholders to optimize their supply chain processes. This subchapter explores the importance of collaboration in supply chain management and its impact on the field of industrial engineering.

Collaboration in supply chain management refers to the active involvement of all participants, including suppliers, manufacturers, distributors, retailers, and even customers, in the decision-making process. By working together, these stakeholders can streamline operations, enhance efficiency, and improve overall performance.

One of the key benefits of collaboration is increased visibility across the supply chain. When all participants share information, data, and insights, they gain a holistic view of the entire value chain. This visibility enables better forecasting, inventory management, and demand planning, leading to reduced costs and improved customer satisfaction. For industrial engineers, collaboration provides a wealth of data and real-time information, which can be analyzed to optimize processes, identify bottlenecks, and drive continuous improvement.

Moreover, collaboration fosters innovation and promotes the exchange of ideas among supply chain partners. By pooling resources, knowledge, and expertise, organizations can develop innovative solutions to common challenges. For industrial engineers, collaboration opens up opportunities for cross-functional problem-solving, enabling them to leverage diverse perspectives and find creative solutions that enhance the efficiency and effectiveness of supply chain operations.

Collaboration also plays a crucial role in risk management. By sharing information about potential disruptions, such as natural disasters, political instability, or supplier issues, organizations can collectively develop contingency plans and mitigate the impact of these risks. Industrial engineers can contribute to this process by analyzing data and designing robust supply chain networks that are resilient to various disruptions.

In conclusion, collaboration is of utmost importance in supply chain management. It enables organizations to achieve greater visibility, enhance innovation, and effectively manage risks. For industrial engineers, collaboration provides a platform to leverage data, optimize processes, and drive operational excellence. As the field of supply chain management continues to evolve, collaboration will remain a critical success factor for organizations and industrial engineers alike.

Building Strong Supplier Relationships

In today's highly competitive business landscape, maintaining strong supplier relationships is crucial for the success of any organization. Effective supply chain management not only involves managing the flow of goods and services from suppliers to customers but also requires fostering strong relationships with suppliers. This subchapter explores the importance of building strong supplier relationships and provides practical strategies for industrial engineering professionals to enhance their supply chain management practices.

Developing strong supplier relationships offers numerous benefits to organizations. Firstly, it promotes better communication and collaboration between buyers and suppliers. By establishing open lines of communication, industrial engineering professionals can gain valuable insights into suppliers' capabilities, production processes, and potential areas of improvement. This knowledge can be leveraged to streamline operations, reduce costs, and drive innovation.

Secondly, strong supplier relationships enable organizations to build trust and reliability. When suppliers feel valued and appreciated, they are more likely to prioritize the organization's needs and provide high-quality products and services consistently. This, in turn, minimizes disruptions in the supply chain, reduces lead times, and enhances customer satisfaction.

To build and maintain strong supplier relationships, industrial engineering professionals should adopt several key strategies. Firstly, they should prioritize regular and transparent communication with suppliers. This involves sharing information about organizational goals, expectations, and performance metrics. Moreover, it is essential to involve suppliers early in the product development process to ensure their expertise and input are utilized effectively.

Industrial engineering professionals should also focus on establishing mutual goals and objectives with suppliers. By aligning their interests, organizations and suppliers can work together towards shared success. This can be achieved through mutually beneficial agreements, such as long-term contracts and collaborative projects, which promote commitment and loyalty.

Furthermore, organizations should invest in supplier development programs. These programs aim to enhance suppliers' capabilities, quality standards, and process efficiencies. By offering training, mentoring, and support, industrial engineering professionals can help suppliers improve their performance, thus benefiting both parties.

In conclusion, building strong supplier relationships is a critical aspect of effective supply chain management. Industrial engineering professionals should recognize the importance of open communication, trust, and collaboration in fostering successful partnerships with suppliers. By implementing strategies such as regular communication, shared objectives, and supplier development programs, organizations can enhance their supply chains, reduce costs, and achieve long-term success in the industrial engineering industry.

Collaborative Planning, Forecasting, and Replenishment (CPFR)

In today's rapidly evolving business landscape, effective supply chain management is crucial for success. One of the key strategies that has emerged in recent years is Collaborative Planning, Forecasting, and Replenishment (CPFR). This subchapter aims to introduce CPFR as a powerful tool for optimizing supply chain operations and improving overall performance.

CPFR is a collaborative approach that brings together suppliers, manufacturers, distributors, and retailers to jointly plan, forecast, and replenish inventory. It is based on the principle that by sharing information and working together, all parties can benefit from improved demand forecasting accuracy, reduced inventory levels, and enhanced customer satisfaction.

Industrial engineering professionals, in particular, can greatly benefit from implementing CPFR in their organizations. By leveraging their expertise in process optimization and system design, they can help streamline and integrate the collaborative planning process, ensuring maximum efficiency and effectiveness.

The CPFR process starts with collaborative planning, where all stakeholders come together to define their objectives, set performance metrics, and establish a framework for decision-making. By aligning their goals and strategies, partners can eliminate inefficiencies and better respond to market demands.

Next, collaborative forecasting involves sharing data and information to develop accurate demand forecasts. This step relies on advanced analytics and statistical models to analyze historical data, market trends, and other relevant factors. Industrial engineering professionals can contribute by designing and implementing forecasting algorithms and systems that leverage the latest technological advancements.

Finally, collaborative replenishment focuses on optimizing inventory levels and ensuring timely product availability. Through real-time sharing of information, partners can adjust and synchronize their production and distribution plans, minimizing stockouts and excess inventory. Industrial engineers can play a crucial role in designing robust inventory management systems that balance cost-efficiency with customer service objectives.

CPFR offers numerous benefits, including improved product availability, reduced lead times, and lower costs throughout the supply chain. By fostering collaboration and information sharing, it also helps build trust and stronger relationships among supply chain partners.

In conclusion, CPFR is a powerful strategy that can revolutionize supply chain operations and deliver exceptional results. Industrial engineering professionals can leverage their expertise to design and implement effective CPFR systems, helping organizations achieve maximum efficiency, cost savings, and customer satisfaction. By embracing the principles of collaboration and information sharing, businesses can unlock the true potential of their supply chains and deliver success in today's competitive marketplace.

Supply Chain Integration and Coordination

In today's interconnected world, the success of any business heavily relies on its ability to effectively manage its supply chain. Supply chain integration and coordination play a pivotal role in ensuring the smooth flow of goods and services from suppliers to end consumers. This subchapter aims to provide an in-depth understanding of the importance of supply chain integration and coordination, particularly for the audience interested in industrial engineering.

Supply chain integration refers to the collaboration between various stakeholders, such as suppliers, manufacturers, distributors, and retailers, to streamline the flow of products and information. By integrating their operations, companies can reduce lead times, minimize costs, and enhance customer satisfaction. Industrial engineers, who are responsible for optimizing complex systems, play a crucial role in designing and implementing integrated supply chains. They use their expertise to identify bottlenecks, streamline processes, and improve overall efficiency.

Coordination within the supply chain is equally vital. It involves aligning the activities of different entities to ensure that they work together harmoniously. Effective coordination ensures that all parties are on the same page regarding production schedules, inventory levels, and customer demands. Industrial engineers with their knowledge of systems optimization can help design coordination mechanisms, such as shared information systems, regular communication channels, and collaborative decision-making processes.

The benefits of supply chain integration and coordination are numerous. Firstly, it reduces uncertainty and increases responsiveness. By sharing information and coordinating activities, companies can respond more effectively to changes in demand or disruptions in the supply chain. Secondly, integration and coordination enable companies to achieve economies of scale and reduce costs. By aggregating demand and optimizing production schedules, companies can minimize inventory levels and transportation costs. Finally, integration and coordination enhance customer satisfaction as companies can provide faster delivery times, accurate information, and a seamless customer experience.

Industrial engineers, in particular, can contribute significantly to achieving supply chain integration and coordination. Their skills in process optimization, data analysis, and systems design are essential for identifying areas of improvement and implementing effective solutions. By embracing the principles of supply chain integration and coordination, industrial engineers can help businesses deliver success by increasing efficiency, reducing costs, and satisfying customer demands.

In conclusion, supply chain integration and coordination are fundamental concepts in effective supply chain management. Industrial engineers play a crucial role in designing and implementing integrated supply chains through their expertise in systems optimization. By embracing these principles, companies can reduce costs, enhance customer satisfaction, and respond more effectively to market changes. This subchapter aims to provide industrial engineering professionals with the knowledge and tools necessary to succeed in the dynamic and interconnected world of supply chain management.

Chapter 9: Future Trends and Innovations in Supply Chain Management

Industry 4.0 and the Digital Supply Chain

In the modern era of technological advancements, the concept of Industry 4.0 has emerged as a revolutionary force, transforming the landscape of industrial engineering and supply chain management. The integration of digital technologies into the traditional supply chain processes has given birth to the concept of the digital supply chain, which holds immense potential for enhancing productivity, efficiency, and profitability.

The digital supply chain refers to the utilization of cutting-edge technologies such as artificial intelligence, machine learning, big data analytics, and the Internet of Things (IoT) to create a seamless and interconnected network of supply chain activities. This integration enables real-time visibility, actionable insights, and optimized decision-making, leading to enhanced operational performance and customer satisfaction.

One of the key benefits of Industry 4.0 and the digital supply chain is the ability to gain end-to-end visibility across the entire supply chain. Traditionally, supply chain managers faced challenges in tracking and monitoring the movement of goods and materials from suppliers to customers. However, with the advent of digital technologies, real-time tracking and monitoring of shipments have become a reality. This enhanced visibility allows for proactive management of potential bottlenecks, delays, and disruptions, ensuring smooth and efficient operations.

Furthermore, the digital supply chain enables intelligent demand forecasting and inventory management. By leveraging advanced analytics and machine learning algorithms, supply chain managers can accurately predict customer demand patterns and optimize inventory levels accordingly. This not only reduces the risk of stockouts and overstocking but also minimizes costs associated with storage and carrying excess inventory.

Another significant advantage of Industry 4.0 and the digital supply chain is the ability to facilitate seamless collaboration and information sharing among stakeholders. With cloud-based platforms and digital communication tools, suppliers, manufacturers, and customers can exchange real-time data, collaborate on product design and development, and streamline order fulfillment processes. This enables faster response times, customization, and improved overall supply chain efficiency.

In conclusion, Industry 4.0 and the digital supply chain have revolutionized the field of industrial engineering and supply chain management. By harnessing the power of digital technologies, organizations can achieve unprecedented levels of visibility, efficiency, and customer satisfaction. The digital supply chain represents the future of supply chain management, and those who embrace it will undoubtedly stay ahead of the competition in this fast-paced, technology-driven world.

Artificial Intelligence and Machine Learning in Supply Chain

Artificial Intelligence (AI) and Machine Learning (ML) have revolutionized various industries, and the field of supply chain management is no exception. In this subchapter, we will explore the incredible potential of AI and ML in optimizing supply chain processes, improving efficiency, and delivering success in the field of industrial engineering.

Supply chain management involves the coordination and integration of various activities, from sourcing raw materials to delivering the final product to customers. This complex process often faces challenges such as unpredictable demand, inventory management, and logistics planning. AI and ML technologies offer innovative solutions to tackle these challenges effectively.

One of the key applications of AI and ML in supply chain management is demand forecasting. By analyzing historical data, market trends, and customer behavior patterns, AI algorithms can accurately predict future demand. This enables companies to optimize their inventory levels, reduce stockouts, and avoid excess inventory, ultimately improving customer satisfaction and reducing costs.

ML algorithms also play a crucial role in optimizing logistics and transportation. By analyzing real-time data such as traffic conditions, weather forecasts, and transportation costs, AI-powered systems can determine the most efficient routes for delivery trucks, optimize load distribution, and minimize transportation costs. This not only enhances operational efficiency but also reduces environmental impact by minimizing fuel consumption and carbon emissions.

AI and ML also enable predictive maintenance, a proactive approach to equipment maintenance. By analyzing sensor data and historical maintenance records, algorithms can predict when a machine is likely to fail. This allows companies to schedule maintenance activities in advance, minimizing downtime and preventing costly breakdowns.

Additionally, AI and ML algorithms can be used to optimize supplier selection and manage supplier relationships. By analyzing supplier data such as performance metrics, delivery times, and quality ratings, companies can make informed decisions about supplier selection and negotiate better terms. This helps in building strong partnerships and ensuring a reliable supply chain.

In conclusion, the integration of AI and ML in supply chain management offers tremendous opportunities for industrial engineers to optimize processes, reduce costs, and deliver success. By leveraging these technologies, companies can achieve higher efficiency, improved customer satisfaction, and a competitive edge in the market. Embracing AI and ML in supply chain management is no longer an option but a necessity for every industrial engineering professional seeking to stay ahead in today's fast-paced and dynamic business environment.

Blockchain Technology in Supply Chain Management

In recent years, blockchain technology has emerged as a revolutionary tool with the potential to transform various industries, including supply chain management. With its decentralized and transparent nature, blockchain offers unique solutions for the challenges faced by supply chain professionals. This subchapter explores the applications and benefits of blockchain technology in supply chain management, shedding light on how it can revolutionize the field of industrial engineering.

Blockchain technology is essentially a digital ledger that records and verifies transactions in a secure and transparent manner. In the context of supply chain management, this technology enables the creation of an immutable and tamper-proof record of every transaction, creating a transparent and auditable supply chain ecosystem. This transparency is particularly important in industries where traceability and accountability are crucial, such as pharmaceuticals, food, and automotive.

One of the key benefits of blockchain technology in supply chain management is enhanced traceability. By recording every transaction on the blockchain, companies can easily track the movement of goods from their origin to the end consumer. This not only reduces the risk of counterfeit products but also allows for quick identification and resolution of any issues that may arise during the supply chain process. Industrial engineers can leverage this traceability to optimize supply chain processes, identify bottlenecks, and improve overall efficiency.

Another advantage of blockchain technology in supply chain management is increased trust and security. With traditional supply chain systems, trust is often an issue, as multiple parties are involved in the process, each with their own systems and databases. Blockchain technology eliminates the need for intermediaries, as all participants have access to the same, decentralized ledger. This ensures that all parties involved in the supply chain have access to accurate and up-to-date information, reducing the risk of fraud and errors.

Furthermore, blockchain technology enables the creation of smart contracts, which are self-executing contracts with predefined rules and conditions. These smart contracts can automate various aspects of the supply chain, such as payment processing, quality control, and compliance verification. Industrial engineers can leverage the capabilities of smart contracts to streamline supply chain operations, reduce costs, and eliminate manual errors.

In conclusion, blockchain technology has the potential to revolutionize supply chain management in the field of industrial engineering. By providing enhanced traceability, increased trust and security, and the ability to automate processes through smart contracts, blockchain technology can optimize supply chain operations, improve efficiency, and ultimately deliver success in the industrial engineering sector. Whether you are a supply chain professional or an industrial engineering enthusiast, understanding and embracing blockchain technology will undoubtedly be a key factor in driving future success in the evolving supply chain landscape.

Predictive Analytics and Big Data in Supply Chain Optimization

In today's highly competitive business landscape, the key to success lies in effective supply chain management. Industrial Engineering professionals play a crucial role in optimizing supply chain operations, ensuring timely delivery of products and services, and maximizing profitability. To achieve these goals, harnessing the power of predictive analytics and big data has become indispensable.

Predictive analytics is a field of data analysis that uses historical and real-time data to make accurate predictions about future events or trends. By applying predictive analytics techniques to supply chain management, industrial engineers can gain valuable insights into customer demand patterns, market trends, and potential disruptions. This enables them to make informed decisions and take proactive measures to ensure smooth operations and customer satisfaction.

Big data refers to the vast amount of structured and unstructured data generated by various sources, such as customer transactions, social media interactions, and sensor readings. By utilizing advanced analytics tools and technologies, industrial engineers can analyze this data to identify patterns, trends, and anomalies. This helps them identify areas of improvement, optimize resource allocation, and streamline supply chain processes.

One of the primary benefits of predictive analytics and big data in supply chain optimization is the ability to enhance demand forecasting accuracy. By analyzing historical sales data, customer preferences, and external factors like weather conditions, industrial engineers can accurately predict future demand patterns. This enables them to optimize inventory levels, reduce stockouts, and minimize carrying costs while meeting customer demands effectively.

Moreover, predictive analytics and big data can also help in identifying potential risks and disruptions in the supply chain. By monitoring real-time data from various sources, such as weather reports, transportation systems, and supplier performance metrics, industrial engineers can detect any potential bottlenecks or delays. This allows them to take proactive measures, such as finding alternative suppliers or rerouting shipments, to minimize the impact on the overall supply chain.

Furthermore, by leveraging big data analytics, industrial engineers can optimize production schedules and resource utilization. By analyzing data related to machine performance, production processes, and employee productivity, they can identify inefficiencies and make data-driven decisions to improve operational efficiency. This leads to cost savings, increased productivity, and improved overall performance.

In conclusion, predictive analytics and big data are revolutionizing the field of supply chain optimization for industrial engineers. By harnessing the power of advanced analytics techniques and leveraging vast amounts of data, they can make accurate predictions, proactively mitigate risks, and optimize supply chain processes. This ultimately leads to improved customer satisfaction, increased profitability, and a competitive edge in today's dynamic business environment.

Chapter 10: Case Studies in Effective Supply Chain Management

Successful Supply Chain Management Practices in the Retail Industry

Introduction:
In today's fast-paced retail industry, effective supply chain management is crucial for the success and growth of businesses. This subchapter explores the key practices that have been proven successful in managing supply chains within the retail sector. Whether you are a business owner, a supply chain professional, or a student of industrial engineering, understanding and implementing these practices can significantly enhance your knowledge and expertise.

1. Collaboration and Partnerships: Successful supply chain management in the retail industry relies on strong collaboration and partnerships with various stakeholders. Retailers must work closely with suppliers, manufacturers, distributors, and logistics providers to ensure a smooth flow of products and information. By fostering strong relationships, sharing data, and aligning goals, retailers can reduce lead times, minimize stockouts, and improve overall customer satisfaction.

2. Demand Forecasting and Inventory Management: Accurate demand forecasting is vital in the retail industry to avoid excess inventory or stockouts. By leveraging historical data, market trends, and advanced analytics, retailers can forecast demand more accurately and optimize their inventory levels. This practice helps reduce carrying costs, minimize waste, and improve cash flow.

3. Efficient Transportation and Logistics: In the retail industry, timely delivery of products to customers'

doorsteps is crucial. Implementing efficient transportation and logistics practices, such as route optimization, real-time tracking, and cross-docking, can significantly enhance supply chain performance. Retailers can benefit from reduced transportation costs, improved delivery speed, and increased customer satisfaction.

4. Technology Adoption:
The retail industry has witnessed a technological revolution in recent years, and successful retailers have embraced these advancements in supply chain management. By leveraging technologies such as artificial intelligence, internet of things, and big data analytics, retailers can gain real-time visibility into their supply chains, automate processes, and make data-driven decisions. Technology adoption enhances supply chain efficiency, reduces costs, and improves forecasting accuracy.

5. Continuous Improvement and Agility:
Retail supply chains are constantly evolving, and successful retailers focus on continuous improvement and agility. By regularly evaluating and optimizing processes, identifying bottlenecks, and embracing new strategies, retailers can stay ahead of the competition. Embracing an agile mindset allows retailers to quickly adapt to changing market dynamics, customer preferences, and emerging trends.

Conclusion:
Successful supply chain management practices are essential for retailers in the ever-evolving retail industry. By implementing collaboration and partnerships, effective demand forecasting, efficient transportation and logistics, technology adoption, and continuous improvement, retailers can optimize their supply chains and achieve sustainable growth. Whether you are an industrial engineering professional or simply interested in the retail industry, understanding

and implementing these practices will undoubtedly contribute to your success.

Supply Chain Excellence in Manufacturing Sector

In today's fast-paced and globalized world, achieving supply chain excellence has become a crucial aspect of success for any manufacturing sector. The ability to effectively manage the flow of materials, information, and resources from suppliers to customers has become a key differentiator in gaining a competitive edge. This subchapter explores the fundamental principles and strategies that drive supply chain excellence in the manufacturing sector, providing valuable insights for professionals and enthusiasts in the field of industrial engineering.

Supply chain excellence in the manufacturing sector begins with a deep understanding of the entire value chain and its interdependencies. From sourcing raw materials to delivering finished products, every step must be optimized to ensure efficiency and cost-effectiveness. This requires a comprehensive approach that incorporates various elements such as demand forecasting, inventory management, production planning, and logistics.

One of the core principles of supply chain excellence is collaboration. Effective collaboration between suppliers, manufacturers, and customers is vital to streamline processes and minimize disruptions. This can be achieved through the implementation of advanced technologies, such as cloud-based platforms that enable real-time data sharing and visibility across the supply chain. By fostering strong relationships and open communication, manufacturers can respond quickly to changes in demand and customer preferences, ultimately enhancing customer satisfaction.

Another crucial aspect of achieving supply chain excellence is continuous improvement. Manufacturers must constantly evaluate their processes, identify bottlenecks, and implement innovative solutions to enhance efficiency. This could involve adopting lean manufacturing techniques, implementing automation and robotics, or leveraging data analytics to optimize production and reduce waste. By embracing a culture of continuous improvement, manufacturers can stay ahead of the competition and adapt to changing market dynamics.

Furthermore, supply chain resilience is paramount in today's unpredictable business environment. Manufacturers must proactively identify and mitigate risks, such as supply disruptions, natural disasters, or geopolitical uncertainties. This can be achieved by diversifying supplier networks, creating backup plans, and investing in robust contingency strategies. By building resilience into the supply chain, manufacturers can ensure continuity of operations and minimize the impact of disruptions on customer satisfaction and profitability.

In conclusion, achieving supply chain excellence in the manufacturing sector is a complex and multifaceted endeavor. It requires a deep understanding of the value chain, effective collaboration, continuous improvement, and resilience. By embracing these principles and adopting innovative strategies, manufacturers can optimize their operations, enhance customer satisfaction, and ultimately drive success in today's competitive landscape. This subchapter serves as a valuable resource for industrial engineering professionals and anyone interested in understanding the power of effective supply chain management.

Supply Chain Innovations in E-commerce and Online Retail

In today's digital age, e-commerce and online retail have become increasingly popular among consumers worldwide. The convenience of shopping from the comfort of our homes, along with the ability to access a wide range of products and services, has revolutionized the way we shop. However, behind the scenes, supply chain innovations play a crucial role in ensuring the smooth functioning of these e-commerce and online retail platforms.

One of the key supply chain innovations in e-commerce and online retail is the implementation of advanced inventory management systems. With the help of real-time data analytics and predictive algorithms, these systems enable retailers to optimize their inventory levels, reduce stockouts, and minimize holding costs. By having accurate and up-to-date information about product demand, retailers can improve their order fulfillment rates and enhance the overall customer experience.

Another significant innovation in this realm is the adoption of automated warehousing and fulfillment centers. With the increasing volume of online orders, traditional manual processes are no longer feasible. Automated systems, such as robotic picking and sorting, not only streamline the order fulfillment process but also reduce labor costs and increase efficiency. By leveraging cutting-edge technologies like artificial intelligence and machine learning, these systems can handle large volumes of orders accurately and at a much faster pace.

Furthermore, the integration of supply chain management systems with customer relationship management (CRM) platforms has become a game-changer for e-commerce and online retail. By connecting order management, inventory, and customer data, retailers can gain valuable insights into customer behavior, preferences, and buying patterns. This information allows them to personalize marketing campaigns, offer tailored promotions, and provide a more personalized shopping experience. Ultimately, this integration leads to higher customer satisfaction and increased customer loyalty.

In addition to these innovations, supply chain visibility and transparency have become paramount in e-commerce and online retail. Customers want to know the status of their orders, from the moment they place it until it arrives at their doorstep. Advanced tracking technologies, such as GPS and RFID, enable real-time tracking and tracing of shipments, providing customers with accurate delivery times and updates. This increased visibility not only enhances the customer experience but also allows retailers to identify potential bottlenecks and optimize their logistics operations.

In conclusion, supply chain innovations in e-commerce and online retail have revolutionized the way we shop and have become essential for the success of these platforms. From advanced inventory management systems to automated warehousing and fulfillment centers, these innovations optimize operational efficiency, enhance customer experience, and drive overall business growth. As e-commerce continues to evolve, it is crucial for retailers to stay abreast of these innovations and leverage them to stay competitive in the digital marketplace.

Global Supply Chain Management in Multinational Corporations

In today's interconnected world, multinational corporations (MNCs) play a crucial role in shaping the global economy. These companies have expanded their operations beyond domestic borders and now operate in multiple countries, requiring effective management of their supply chains to ensure smooth operations and maximize profits. This subchapter explores the concept of global supply chain management in MNCs and its significance in the field of industrial engineering.

Global supply chain management refers to the coordination and optimization of all activities involved in the procurement, production, and distribution of goods and services across multiple countries. MNCs face unique challenges in managing their supply chains due to geographical, cultural, and regulatory differences. Hence, it is essential for industrial engineers and professionals in the field to understand the intricacies of global supply chain management to drive success in MNCs.

One of the key aspects of global supply chain management is ensuring a seamless flow of resources and information across borders. This involves selecting reliable suppliers, managing transportation networks, and implementing efficient inventory management systems. Industrial engineers play a vital role in designing and implementing these systems, using their expertise to optimize processes, reduce costs, and improve overall supply chain performance.

Additionally, MNCs must navigate complex legal and regulatory frameworks when operating in different countries. Industrial engineers need to be well-versed in international trade regulations, customs requirements, and local laws to ensure compliance and avoid disruptions in the supply chain. They must also account for cultural differences, language barriers, and varying business practices when collaborating with suppliers and partners across borders.

Effective global supply chain management enables MNCs to gain a competitive advantage by leveraging economies of scale, accessing new markets, and reducing costs. By streamlining processes and enhancing collaboration among various stakeholders, industrial engineers contribute to the overall success of MNCs in today's globalized business environment.

In conclusion, global supply chain management is a critical aspect of multinational corporations' operations in the modern world. Industrial engineers play a pivotal role in designing and managing efficient supply chains that span multiple countries. Their knowledge and expertise in optimizing processes, navigating legal frameworks, and fostering collaboration are vital for the success of MNCs in today's global marketplace. By understanding the intricacies of global supply chain management, industrial engineering professionals can drive growth and deliver success for multinational corporations worldwide.

Chapter 11: Conclusion and Key Takeaways

Recap of Important Concepts Covered in the Book

In the book "Delivering Success: The Power of Effective Supply Chain Management," we have explored a wide range of important concepts related to supply chain management. This subchapter serves as a recap of these key concepts, providing a concise summary for the benefit of everyone, particularly those in the niche of industrial engineering.

Supply chain management is the coordination of all activities involved in the production and delivery of goods and services. It encompasses various elements such as sourcing, procurement, production, warehousing, logistics, and customer service. One of the fundamental concepts discussed in the book is the importance of aligning these activities to achieve operational efficiency and customer satisfaction.

Effective supply chain management requires a holistic approach, considering both internal and external factors. It involves collaboration and communication between different stakeholders, including suppliers, manufacturers, distributors, retailers, and customers. The book emphasizes the significance of building strong relationships and leveraging technology to enhance transparency, streamline processes, and optimize decision-making.

Another crucial concept explored is the need for flexibility and agility in supply chain operations. In today's dynamic business environment, companies must be able to adapt quickly to changes in demand, market conditions, and disruptions. The book discusses strategies for achieving flexibility, such as inventory optimization, demand forecasting, and agile manufacturing.

Furthermore, the book delves into the concept of sustainability in supply chain management. As industrial engineering professionals, it is essential to understand the environmental and social impact of supply chain activities. The book highlights the importance of implementing sustainable practices, such as green logistics, waste reduction, and ethical sourcing. These practices not only contribute to corporate social responsibility but also improve cost-efficiency and reputation.

Lastly, the book stresses the significance of continuous improvement in supply chain management. Through the use of performance metrics, data analytics, and benchmarking, companies can identify areas for enhancement and implement strategies to drive operational excellence. The book provides insights into various improvement methodologies, including lean management, Six Sigma, and total quality management.

In conclusion, "Delivering Success: The Power of Effective Supply Chain Management" covers a wide range of essential concepts for everyone interested in supply chain management, especially those in the niche of industrial engineering. By understanding and applying these concepts, individuals and organizations can achieve operational efficiency, customer satisfaction, sustainability, and continuous improvement in their supply chain operations.

Lessons Learned and Key Takeaways for Effective Supply Chain Management

In today's rapidly changing business landscape, the role of effective supply chain management has become paramount. It is no longer just about moving goods from one point to another, but rather a strategic function that integrates various aspects of the business, from procurement to distribution. In this subchapter, we will explore some crucial lessons learned and key takeaways for effectively managing the supply chain, with a particular focus on the industrial engineering niche.

Lesson 1: Collaboration is the Key
One of the critical lessons learned is the importance of collaboration among all stakeholders in the supply chain. Industrial engineers must actively engage with suppliers, manufacturers, distributors, and customers to ensure seamless coordination. By fostering strong relationships, sharing information, and aligning goals, efficiency and effectiveness can be maximized.

Lesson 2: Embrace Technology and Innovation
The digital revolution has transformed supply chain management. Industrial engineers need to embrace technological advancements such as automation, artificial intelligence, and data analytics to optimize processes. By incorporating innovative solutions, organizations can enhance visibility, streamline operations, and gain a competitive edge in today's fast-paced environment.

Lesson 3: Resilience and Risk Management
Supply chains are vulnerable to various risks, including natural disasters, political instability, and economic downturns. Industrial engineers must adopt a proactive approach to identify potential risks

and develop contingency plans to mitigate their impact. Resilience and risk management strategies should be integrated into the entire supply chain to ensure continuity and minimize disruptions.

Lesson 4: Sustainability and Ethical Practices
In recent years, the focus on sustainable and ethical practices has gained significant momentum. Industrial engineers should consider the environmental and social implications of their supply chain decisions. By implementing green initiatives, reducing waste, and promoting fair labor practices, organizations can create a positive brand image, attract socially responsible customers, and enhance long-term profitability.

Key Takeaways:
1. Collaboration is crucial for effective supply chain management.
2. Embrace technology and innovation to optimize processes.
3. Develop resilience and risk management strategies to minimize disruptions.
4. Implement sustainable and ethical practices for long-term success.

In conclusion, effective supply chain management is a critical aspect of business success, particularly in the industrial engineering niche. By adopting the lessons learned and key takeaways mentioned above, organizations can build robust and resilient supply chains that drive efficiency, innovation, and sustainability.

Final Thoughts on the Power of Effective Supply Chain Management

In today's fast-paced and highly competitive business environment, effective supply chain management holds the key to success for organizations across various industries. The power of a well-designed and efficiently executed supply chain cannot be overstated. It has the potential to transform businesses and drive them towards unprecedented levels of success. As we come to the end of this book, it is essential to reflect on the crucial role of supply chain management and its impact on industrial engineering.

Supply chain management is not just about moving goods from one point to another; it encompasses a holistic approach that involves strategic planning, coordination, and collaboration among various stakeholders involved in the process. From raw material sourcing to product delivery, every step in the supply chain must be carefully orchestrated to ensure seamless operations and customer satisfaction.

For industrial engineers, understanding and optimizing supply chain management is of utmost importance. By effectively managing the flow of materials, information, and finances, industrial engineers can drive efficiency, reduce costs, and enhance overall productivity. The ability to identify bottlenecks, streamline processes, and implement innovative solutions can significantly impact an organization's bottom line.

In today's globalized economy, effective supply chain management is even more critical. With the rise of e-commerce and the increasing demand for rapid delivery, organizations must be agile and responsive to changing market dynamics. By leveraging technology and embracing digitalization, industrial engineers can harness the power of data analytics, artificial intelligence, and automation to optimize supply chain processes, reduce lead times, and improve customer satisfaction.

Moreover, effective supply chain management plays a crucial role in sustainability initiatives. As businesses strive to reduce their carbon footprint and contribute to a greener future, industrial engineers can design eco-friendly supply chains that minimize waste, energy consumption, and environmental impact. By adopting sustainable practices, organizations can not only enhance their reputation but also reduce costs and improve long-term profitability.

In conclusion, effective supply chain management is a powerful tool that can revolutionize businesses across all industries. Industrial engineers play a vital role in optimizing supply chain processes, driving efficiency, and ensuring customer satisfaction. By embracing technology, leveraging data analytics, and promoting sustainability, organizations can unlock the true potential of their supply chain and achieve unprecedented success in today's competitive marketplace.

www.ingramcontent.com/pod-product-compliance
Lightning Source LLC
LaVergne TN
LVHW051957060526
838201LV00059B/3691